A Gardener's Nosegay:

Ripe Wisdom, Perennial Poesy, and Wild Folklore

A Gardener's Nosegay:

Ripe Wisdom, Perennial Poesy, and Wild Folklore

Hand-picked by Jude Patterson

BARNES & NOBLE BOOKS
NEW YORK

The quotes in this book have been drawn from many sources, and are assumed to be accurate as quoted in their previously published forms. Although every effort has been made to verify the quotes and sources, the publisher cannot guarantee their perfect accuracy.

2003 Barnes & Noble Books

ISBN 0-7607-4064-x

Printed and bound in the United States of America

M 9 8 7 6 5 4 3 2 1

If you would be happy for a day, get drunk.
If you would be happy for a week, take a wife.
If you would be happy for a month, kill your pig.
But if you would be happy all your life, plant
a garden.

—CHINESE PROVERB

AS THE EARTH WHIRLS IN ITS YEARLY DANCE AROUND the sun, gardeners and nature lovers take special pleasure in the changes each season brings. In winter, when roots and seeds sleep under the crusted snow, the gardener is an artist hatching ideas for the coming season. As the days lengthen and the sap starts to rise, a walk in the woods shows signs of spring's rebirth. Soon migrating birds return, and the gardener spends long hours lost in the satisfying work of painting with plants. Amid pruning, hoeing, planting, and weeding, the garden unfolds with balmy bloom. By midsummer, the strengths and weaknesses of the garden plan are obvious—and nature shows her hand.

A garden is a labor of love, an alliance with nature in which nature always has the last word. The gardener becomes a great listener, learning the vagaries of soil, sunlight, and killing frosts, discovering which plants thrive, and those which invite beneficial visitors. Autumn gives the gardener a chance to propose modifications by expunging mistakes, pairing perennials differently, trying new varieties of bulbs. Plants brought indoors brighten the windowsill through winter's respite, and the blanket of fresh snow is a canvas on which to paint dreams of next year's garden.

Like a bouquet from any garden where only a limited number of varieties have room to flourish, *A Gardener's Nosegay: Ripe Wisdom, Perennial Poesy, and Wild Folklore* is but a small sampling of gardening wisdom collected from sources old and new, accented with poetic musings, quaint folk beliefs, and age-old proverbs on weather and the seasons. Whether your garden is a humble potted geranium on a sunny windowsill, a jumble of annuals and perennials in a shade-dappled border, a vegetable patch producing food for the table, or a rambling wilderness filled at every turn with nature's surprises, it is hoped that *A Gardener's Nosegay* spills seeds of happiness throughout your gardening year.

Jude Patterson

January

God Almighty first planted a Garden. And indeed, it is the purest of human pleasures.

—FRANCIS BACON, "Of Gardens," 1625

What was Paradise? but a garden, an orchard of trees and herbs, full of pleasure, and nothing there but delights.

—WILLIAM LAWSON,
The Country Housewife's Garden, 1617

A garden is a delight to the eye and a solace for the soul.

—SA'DI (CA. 1213-92)

There is a saving streak of the primitive in all of us. Every man secretly believes that if he were an Adam, set down in a virgin world, he would not only be able to survive but could also provide well for his Eve and any number of little Cains and Abels.

—EUELL GIBBONS, *Stalking the Wild Asparagus,* 1962

To own a bit of ground, to scratch it with a hoe, to plant seeds, and watch their renewal of life—this is the commonest delight of the race, the most satisfactory thing a man can do.

—CHARLES DUDLEY WARNER,
My Summer in a Garden, 1871

When I go into my garden with a spade, and dig a bed, I feel such an exhilaration and health, that I discover that I have been defrauding myself all this time in letting others do for me what I should have done with my own hands.

—RALPH WALDO EMERSON, speech,
"Man the Reformer," 25 January 1841

For I hold it that the best purpose of a garden is to give delight and to give refreshment of mind, to soothe, to refine, and to lift up the heart in a spirit of praise and thankfulness. It is certain that those who practise gardening in the best ways find it to be so.

—GERTRUDE JEKYLL, *Wood and Garden,* 1899

A garden is a lovesome thing, God wot!

—T. E. BROWN, "My Garden," 1893

I do hold it, in the royal ordering of gardens, there ought to be gardens for all the months in the year; in which severally things of beauty may be then in season.

—FRANCIS BACON, "Of Gardens," 1625

How precious are the flowers of mid-winter! Not the hot-house things, nor even the forced trusses of lilac, . . . but the genuine toughs that for some strange reason elect to display themselves out-of-doors at this time of year.

—VITA SACKVILLE-WEST, *Garden Book,* 1968

A gush of violets along a wood path.

—NATHANIEL HAWTHORNE,
American Notebooks, entry for 23 January 1842

All for each. The winds wander, the snow and rain and dew fall, the earth whirls—all but to prosper a poor lush violet.

—JOHN MUIR, journal, 1873

The sweet scents of a garden are by no means the least of its many delights. Even January brings *Chimonanthus fragrans* [*C. praecox,* wintersweet], one of the sweetest and strongest scented of the year's blooms.... They have no stalks, but if they are floated in a shallow dish of water, they last well for several days, and give off a powerful fragrance in a room.

—GERTRUDE JEKYLL, *Wood and Garden,* 1899

Once while hiking across crusted snow in mid-January, I came on a persimmon tree with many fruits still hanging on. With an appetite sharpened by the long walk in the wintery air, I climbed the tree and stuffed myself with those soft, sugary lumps of goodness. When I could hold no more, I gave all the limbs a good shake then descended and picked up from the crusted snow enough ripe persimmons to fill the plastic bag I always carry in my pocket in order to bring home any unexpected gift which the woodland might offer. The whole family enjoyed the persimmon pudding we had for dessert that evening.

—Euell Gibbons, *Stalking the Wild Asparagus,* 1962

The act of putting into your mouth what the earth has grown is perhaps your most direct interaction with the earth.

—Frances Moore Lappé,
Diet for a Small Planet, 1971

In January the best-known plants are the so-called flowers on the window-panes. To make them flourish your room must be fuggy with vapour; if the air is completely dry you will not raise one poor little needle, not to mention flowers. Then the window must not shut properly: where the wind blows into the window, flowers of ice will grow. They flourish more with poor people than with the rich, because the windows of the rich shut better.

—KAREL ČAPEK, *The Gardener's Year,* 1929

As the Day lengthens the Cold strengthens.

—ENGLISH PROVERB

My "drinking uncle" says that, even during the worst blizzard in January, a glass of Dandelion Wine will bring summer right into the house.

—EUELL GIBBONS, *Stalking the Wild Asparagus,* 1962

A Drunkard cannot meet a Cork
Without a Revery–
And so encountering a Fly
This January Day
Jamaicas of Remembrance stir
That send me reeling in.

–EMILY DICKINSON, "NO. 1628," CA. 1884

ST. AGNES' EVE, 20 JANUARY,
when maidens dream of their future husbands

Into her dream he melted, as the rose
Blendeth its odour with the violet,–
Solution sweet: meantime the frost-wind blows
Like Love's alarum pattering the sharp sleet
Against the window-panes; St. Agnes' moon
hath set.

–JOHN KEATS, "The Eve of St. Agnes," 1820

January is the best time for gardeners. From the window of the attic where I write, the gardens are bare to their bones, neat and clean, nicely edged, weed-free. They are an empty page on which to draw the garden of my dreams.

–SARA STEIN, *My Weeds,* 1988

February

CANDLEMAS DAY, 2 FEBRUARY

If Candlemas Day be sunny and bright,
    winter will have another flight.
If Candlemas Day be cloudy with rain,
    winter is gone and won't come again.

—ENGLISH PROVERB

If in February there be no rain,
'tis neither good for hay nor grain.

—ENGLISH PROVERB

Do not move the markers on the border of the fields.

—AMENEMOPE (11th century B.C.),
The Instructions of Amenemope

This used to be among my prayers–a piece of land not so very large, which would contain a garden, and near the house a spring of ever-flowing water, and beyond these a bit of wood.

–HORACE, *Satires,* 35 B.C.

I often wished that I had clear,
For life, six hundred pounds a-year,
A handsome house to lodge a friend,
A river at my garden's end,
A terrace walk, and half a rood
Of land, set out to plant a wood.

–JONATHAN SWIFT,
"Imitation of Horace," written 1714

Oh for a lodge in some vast wilderness,
Some boundless contiguity of shade,
Where rumor of oppression and deceit,
Of unsuccessful or successful war,
Might never reach me more.

–WILLIAM COWPER, *The Task,* 1785

The first man who, having fenced in a piece of land, said, "This is mine," and found people naïve enough to believe him, that man was the true founder of civil society.

—JEAN-JACQUES ROUSSEAU,
Discourse upon the Origin and Foundation of the Inequality Among Mankind, 1754

My apple trees will never get across
And eat the cones under his pines, I tell him.
He only says, "Good fences make good
neighbors."

—ROBERT FROST, "Mending Wall," 1914

Plans [for the garden] should be made on the ground to fit the place, and not the place made to suit some plan out of a book.

—WILLIAM ROBINSON, *The Garden Beautiful,* 1907

Consult the Genius of the Place in all;
That tells the Waters or to rise, or fall, . . .
Now breaks or now directs, th' intending Lines;
Paints as you plant, and, as you work, designs.

—ALEXANDER POPE, "To Lord Burlington," 1731

Of bean-flowers I speak not, because they are field flowers. But those which perfume the air most delightfully, not passed by as the rest, but being trodden upon and crushed, are three; that is, burnet, wild-thyme, and watermints. Therefore you are to set whole alleys of them, to have the pleasure when you walk or tread.

–FRANCIS BACON, "Of Gardens," 1625

If you empty the ashtrays while your friends are still smoking, you will be equally bothered by weeds in the yard, and you will be better off with a style of garden that doesn't show them up. . . . [But if] you are a casual housekeeper, go right ahead and lay out brick terraces and clipped walks, for you will enjoy them even when you know that you ought to do something about their appearance.

–THALASSA CRUSO,
Making Things Grow Outdoors, 1976

Nor am I displeased with the placing of ridiculous Statues in Gardens, provided they have nothing in them obscene.

–LEON BATTISTA ALBERTI, *De Re Ædificatoria,* 1485

Should you ever find yourself lost in [a maze], choose either the right or the left wall and follow its every turning. You can't fail to emerge.

—ELEANOR PERÉNYI, *Green Thoughts,* 1981

ST. VALENTINE'S DAY, 14 FEBRUARY

And I will make thee beds of roses
And a thousand fragrant posies,
A cap of flowers, and a kirtle
Embroidered all with leaves of myrtle; . . .
And if these pleasures may thee move,
Come live with me, and be my love.

—CHRISTOPHER MARLOWE,
"The Passionate Shepherd to His Love," 1599

First a howling blizzard woke us,
Then the rain came down to soak us,
And now before the eye can focus—
Crocus.

—LILJA ROGERS, 1964

For many years I was self-appointed inspector of snowstorms and rainstorms, and did my duty faithfully, though I never received one cent for it.

–HENRY DAVID THOREAU,
journal, 22 February 1845-47

Wild garlic is the first sign of spring. Crowding past brown grass, pushing aside dead leaves, braving dismal sog and dirty snow, its slender, tender, blue-green blades stand here ten inches high before February is out. It's up before the crocuses, before snowdrops even, off to a running start in maple-sugar time.

–SARA STEIN, *My Weeds,* 1988

During some of the warm days that nearly always come towards the end of February, if one knows where to look in some sunny, sheltered corner of a hazel copse, there will be sure to be some Primroses, and the first scent of the year's first Primrose is no small pleasure.

–GERTRUDE JEKYLL, *Wood and Garden,* 1899

I must own that I would do almost anything, and grow almost anything, for the sake of a fragrance.

—REGINALD FARRER, *In a Yorkshire Garden,* 1909

The secret of good gardening: choose always the best of any variety you want to grow.

—VITA SACKVILLE-WEST, *Garden Book,* 1968

March

On the first of March, the crows begin to search.

—ENGLISH PROVERB

So many mists in March, so many frosts in May.

—ENGLISH PROVERB

When the wind is in the east, 'tis neither good for man nor beast.

—ENGLISH PROVERB

I am become a great florist, and shrub-doctor.

—WILLIAM COWPER, letter, 14 March 1767

Popular proverbs mostly prophesy unhappy and gloomy things. The existence of gardeners who every year, in spite of these bad experiences with the weather, welcome and unveil the spring is therefore a testimony of the imperishable and miraculous optimism of the human race.

—KAREL ČAPEK, *The Gardener's Year,* 1929

Terrified though we may be of cutting inexpertly into living wood, or of cutting at the wrong time, the most inexperienced amongst us need have no fear in chopping away dead rubbish which Nature herself has discarded. The same applies to those little feeble twiggy growths which will never come to anything and only rob the branch by their small but cumulative filching of the plant's life. Shave them off. Weaklings must be sacrificed, in the hard harsh law of Nature.

—VITA SACKVILLE-WEST, *Garden Book,* 1968

There is a psychological distinction between cutting back and pruning. Pruning is supposed to be for the welfare of the tree or shrub; cutting back is for the satisfaction of the cutter.

–CHRISTOPHER LLOYD,
The Well-Tempered Garden, 1973

I knew an old labourer who died of a rose-prick.... For some time I did not see him, and when I asked another old countryman, "What's gone o' Master Trussler?" the answer was, "He's dead–died of a canker-bush." The wild Dog-rose is still the "canker" in the speech of the old people, and a thorn or prickle is still a "bush." A Dog-rose prickle had gone deep into the old hedger's hand–a "bush" more or less was nothing to him, but the neglected little wound had become tainted with some impurity, blood-poisoning had set in, and my poor old friend had truly enough "died of a canker-bush."

–GERTRUDE JEKYLL, *Wood and Garden,* 1899

ST. PATRICK'S DAY, 17 MARCH

O Paddy dear, an' did ye hear the news that's
goin' round?
The shamrock is by law forbid to grow on Irish
ground!
No more Saint Patrick's Day we'll keep, his
colour can't be seen,
For there's a cruel law agin the wearin' o' the Green!

–ANONYMOUS

Green how I want you green.
Green wind.
Green branches.

–FEDERICO GARCÍA LORCA,
Romance Sonámbulo, 1924–27

People's backyards are much more interesting than their front gardens, and houses that back on to railways are public benefactors.

–JOHN BETJEMAN, in *Observer,* 20 March 1983

I go among the fields and catch a glimpse of a stoat or a fieldmouse peeping out of the withered grass–The creature hath a purpose and its eyes are bright with it–I go amongst the buildings of a city and I see a man hurrying along–to what? The Creature has a purpose and his eyes are bright with it.

–John Keats, letter, 19 March 1819

I once had a sparrow alight upon my shoulder for a moment while I was hoeing in a village garden, and I felt that I was more distinguished by that circumstance than I should have been by any epaulette I could have worn.

–Henry David Thoreau, *Walden,* 1854

My father must have taught me how to hoe. I think this because he keeps telling me, even though he has been dead two decades now, that I'm doing it left-handed. . . . Whichever way I do it, the arm tires quickly. Then he appears again to tell me that I work too fast, that's why I don't last long. He's right. Mr. Knowlton hoes a slow row.

–Sara Stein, *My Weeds,* 1988

It is no use asking me or any one else how to dig.... Better go and watch a man digging, and then take a spade and try to do it, and go on trying till it comes, and you gain the knack that is to be learnt with all tools, of doubling the power and halving the effort; and meanwhile you will be learning other things, about your own arms and legs and back, and perhaps a little robin will come and give you moral support, and at the same time keep a sharp look-out for any worms you may happen to turn up; and you will find out that there are all sorts of ways of learning, not only from people and books, but from sheer trying.

—GERTRUDE JEKYLL, *Wood and Garden,* 1899

Few lend (but fools)
Their working Tools.

—THOMAS TUSSER,
A Hundreth Good Pointes of Husbandrie, 1557

The best weather instrument yet devised is a pair of human eyes.

—HAROLD M. GIBSON, in *New York Times,*
30 March 1984

To-day, on the 30th of March, at ten o'clock in the morning, the first tiny blossom of forsythia opened. For three days I have been watching its largest bud, a tiny golden pod, so as not to miss this historic moment; it happened while I was looking at the sky to see whether it would rain. To-morrow the twigs of forsythia will be sprinkled all over with golden stars. You simply cannot hold it back.

—KAREL ČAPEK, *The Gardener's Year,* 1929

The gathering in of the clouds with the last rush and dying breath of the wind, and then the regular dripping of twigs and leaves the country o'er, the impression of inward comfort and sociableness, the drenched stubble and trees that drop beads on you as you pass, their dim outline seen through the rain on all sides drooping in sympathy with yourself. These are my undisputed territory.

—HENRY DAVID THOREAU, journal, 30 March 1840

March comes in like a lion, and goes out like a lamb.

—ENGLISH PROVERB

April

If it thunders on All Fools' Day
it brings good crops of corn and hay.

—ENGLISH PROVERB

The first day of spring was once the time for taking the young virgins into the fields, there in dalliance to set an example in fertility for Nature to follow. Now we just set the clock an hour ahead and change the oil in the crankcase.

—E. B. WHITE, *One Man's Meat,* 1944

This day I bestowed too much time in the garden, and thereby was worse able to perform spiritual duties.

—MARGARET HOBY, diary, 6 April 1605

Oh, Adam was a gardener, and God who made
him sees
That half a proper gardener's work is done upon
his knees.

—RUDYARD KIPLING,
"The Glory of the Garden," 1911

What a man needs in gardening is a cast-iron back, with a hinge in it.

—CHARLES DUDLEY WARNER,
My Summer in a Garden, 1871

Those who have had no experience cannot imagine how one's legs are in the way, when there is nothing to stand on; how stupidly long they are if one has to fold them underneath to poke with the finger in the ground; how impossibly short they are if one has to reach to the other side of the bed without treading on a clump of pyrethrum or on the shoots of columbine. If only one could hang in a belt and swim over the beds.

—KAREL ČAPEK, *The Gardener's Year,* 1929

I've noticed something about gardening. You set out to do one thing and pretty soon you're doing something else, which leads to some other thing, and so on. By the end of the day, you look at the shovel stuck in the half-dug rose bed and wonder what on earth you've been doing.

—ANNE RAVER, *Deep in the Green,* 1995

In the spring, at the end of the day, you should smell like dirt.

—MARGARET ATWOOD, "Bluebeard's Egg," 1986

Mud-pies gratify one of our first and best instincts. So long as we are dirty, we are pure.

—CHARLES DUDLEY WARNER,
My Summer in a Garden, 1871

True gardeners cannot bear a glove
Between the sure touch and the tender root.

—MAY SARTON, "As Does New Hampshire," 1967

The first seed that we planted in the spring was sunflower seed. . . . Usually we planted sunflowers only around the edges of a field. The hills were placed eight or nine paces apart; for we never sowed sunflowers thickly. We thought a field surrounded thus by a sparse-sown row of sunflowers, had a handsome appearance.

—BUFFALO BIRD WOMAN, in Gilbert L. Wilson,
Buffalo Bird Woman's Garden, 1917

Let first the onion flourish there,
Rose among roots, the maiden-fair,
Wine-scented and poetic soul
Of the capacious salad bowl.

—ROBERT LOUIS STEVENSON, "To a Gardener," 1887

This is ev'ry cook's opinion, no sav'ry dish
without an onion:
But lest your kissing should be spoil'd, your
onions must be throughly boil'd.

—JONATHAN SWIFT (1667-1745)

To make some snooty little sandwiches for an afternoon tea, butter some thin slices from a small round loaf of rye bread. Make the filling from 1 cup of chopped water cress; ¼ cup of chopped hickory nuts, pecans, or walnuts; some mayonnaise and a little salt. If these sandwiches are to be served at a card party, cut the slices of bread into hearts, diamonds, spades and clubs with cookie cutters.

—EUELL GIBBONS, *Stalking the Wild Asparagus,* 1962

CUCKOO DAY, 14 APRIL, *when migrating birds return*

Spring, the sweet spring, is the year's pleasant
king;
Then blooms each thing, then maids dance in
a ring,
Cold doth not sting, the pretty birds do sing:
Cuckoo, jug-jug, pu-we, to-witta-woo!

—THOMAS NASHE, "Spring," 1600

I shall not ask Jean Jacques Rousseau
If birds confabulate or no.

—WILLIAM COWPER,
"Pairing Time Anticipated," ca. 1794

One swallow does not make a spring; neither does one fine day.

—ARISTOTLE (384-322 B.C.), *Nicomachean Ethics*

Sweet April showers
Do spring May flowers.

—THOMAS TUSSER,
A Hundreth Good Pointes of Husbandrie, 1557

I hate flowers—I paint them because they're cheaper than models and they don't move.

—GEORGIA O'KEEFFE, in *New York Herald Tribune,* 18 April 1954

ARBOR DAY, 22 APRIL

He plants trees to benefit another generation.

—CAECILIUS (220-168 B.C.), *Synephebi*

A tree is made to live in peace in the color of day and in friendship with the sun, the wind and the rain. Its roots plunge in the fat fermentation of the soil, sucking in its elemental humors, its fortifying juices. Trees always seem lost in a great tranquil dream. The dark rising sap makes them groan in the warm afternoons. A tree is a living being that knows the course of the clouds and presses the storms because it is full of birds' nests.

—JACQUES ROUMAIN, *Masters of the Dew,* 1946

May

The month of May was come, when every lusty heart beginneth to blossom, and to bring forth fruit; for like as herbs and trees bring forth fruit and flourish in May, in likewise every lusty heart that is in any manner a lover, springeth and flourisheth in lusty deeds. For it giveth unto all lovers courage, that lusty month of May.

—SIR THOMAS MALORY, *Le Morte d'Arthur,* 1485

The word May is a perfumed word. It is an illuminated initial. It means youth, love, song, and all that is beautiful in life.

—HENRY WADSWORTH LONGFELLOW,
journal, 1 May 1861

My garden is an honest place. Every tree and every vine are incapable of concealment, and tell after two or three months exactly what sort of treatment they have had. The sower may mistake and sow his peas crookedly: the peas make no mistake but come and show his line.

—RALPH WALDO EMERSON, journal, 8 May 1843

Nothing is more pleasant to the eye than green grass kept finely shorn.

—FRANCIS BACON, "Of Gardens," 1625

Consider the many special delights a lawn affords: soft mattress for a creeping baby; worm hatchery for a robin; croquet or badminton court; baseball diamond; restful green perspectives leading the eye to a background of flower border, shrubs, or hedge;... This carpet! What pleasanter surface on which to walk, sit, lie, or even to read Tennyson?

—KATHARINE S. WHITE,
Onward and Upward in the Garden, 1979

I learned to love dandelions when I was a small child. Not only did I enjoy the delicious dandelion greens my mother gathered and prepared, but the bright yellow flower, with its wonderful composite construction, fascinated me. I never believed that spring had really come until I saw the first dandelion in bloom.

—EUELL GIBBONS, *Stalking the Wild Asparagus,* 1962

If the down flies off a Dandelion when there is no wind, it is a sure sign of rain.

—A. STODDARD KULL, *Secrets of Flowers,* 1976

Now 'tis the spring, and weeds are shallow-
rooted;
Suffer them now and they'll o'ergrow the garden.

—WILLIAM SHAKESPEARE, *King Henry VI,* 1592

Oft digging, removing and weeding ye see
Makes hearbs the more wholesome and greater
to be.

—THOMAS TUSSER,
A Hundreth Good Pointes of Husbandrie, 1557

Corn and weeds alike grew rapidly now, and we women of the household were out with our hoes daily, to keep ahead of the weeds... We hoed but once, not very many weeds coming up to bother us afterwards. In my girlhood we were not troubled with mustard and thistles; these weeds have come in with white men.

—BUFFALO BIRD WOMAN, in Gilbert L. Wilson, *Buffalo Bird Woman's Garden,* 1917

Weeding is a delightful occupation, especially after summer rain, when the roots come up clear and clean. One gets to know how many and various are the ways of weeds—as many almost as the moods of human creatures.

—GERTRUDE JEKYLL, *Wood and Garden,* 1899

Nothing is so interesting as weeding. I went crazy over the outdoor work, and had at last to confine myself to the house, or literature must have gone by the board.

—ROBERT LOUIS STEVENSON, letter, 1890

To rip a weed from the earth is satisfying. There is a pale, crackling sound heard in the head and felt in the hand as the tenderest root fibers break from their holdfasts; then a bright, cheery crunch as the clump itself gives way. I like the weightiness of the clump; I like the way the weight lightens as the soil, shaken out, beaten out, spatters its sustenance back to the ground. There is a fine sensation of murder.

—SARA STEIN, *My Weeds*, 1988

If you gently touch a nettle
it'll sting you for your pains;
grasp it like a lad of mettle,
an' as soft as silk remains.

—ENGLISH PROVERB

I learnt from an old farmer a good way of getting rid of a bed of nettles–to thrash them down with a stick every time they grow up. If this is done about three times during the year, the root becomes so much weakened that it is easily forked out, or if the treatment is gone on with, the second year the nettles die.

–GERTRUDE JEKYLL, *Wood and Garden,* 1899

What is a weed? A plant whose virtues have not been discovered.

–RALPH WALDO EMERSON,
Fortune of the Republic, 1878

[Weeds] put nutrients into the soil as well as taking them out, preserve tilth, and some are useful in insect control. The green lacewing, for example, whose larvae devour many pests, itself feeds on the nectar of nettles, lamb's-quarters and dandelions–all of which happen to make delicious soups and salads as well.

–ELEANOR PERÉNYI, *Green Thoughts,* 1981

When in poison ivy's vicinity, I conciliate it, like the Cherokee, by addressing it as "my friend."

—JOHN EASTMAN,
The Book of Forest and Thicket, 1992

Until it has been tamed a hose is an extraordinarily evasive and dangerous beast, for it contorts itself, it jumps, it wriggles, it makes puddles of water, and dives with delight into the mess it has made; then it goes for the man who is going to use it and coils itself round his legs; you must hold it down with your foot, and then it rears and twists round your waist and neck, and while you are fighting with it as with a cobra, the monster turns up its brass mouth and projects a mighty stream of water through the windows on to the curtains which have been recently hung.

—KAREL ČAPEK, *The Gardener's Year,* 1929

The compost heap was behind the potting shed next to the garden and the well. My father tended it lovingly, layered it with soil, turned it with a pitchfork, soaked it with a hose and, when it was done to a turn, crumbly and black, tossed it through a frame of hardware cloth to sieve from it any stem or root that had escaped decay. Then he fed it to his vegetables, grunting and cussing behind a loud, cantankerous machine, the first Rototiller. There was a gardener!

—SARA STEIN, *My Weeds,* 1988

Grass grows very fast. Honey-suckles very fragrant, and most beautiful objects. Columbines make a figure. My white thorn, which hangs over the earth-house, is now one sheet of bloom, and has pendulous boughs down to the ground.

—GILBERT WHITE, journal, 31 May 1792

MEMORIAL DAY, 30 MAY

If ye break faith with us who die
We shall not sleep, though poppies grow
In Flanders fields.

—JOHN MCCRAE, "In Flanders Fields," 1915

June

A dry May and a dripping June brings all things in tune.

—ENGLISH PROVERB

What is one to say about June—the time of perfect young summer, the fulfilment of the promise of the earlier months, and with as yet no sign to remind one that its fresh young beauty will ever fade? For my own part I wander up into the wood and say, "June is here—June is here; thank God for lovely June!"

—GERTRUDE JEKYLL, *Wood and Garden,* 1899

All gardening is landscape-painting.

—ALEXANDER POPE, in Joseph Spence, *Anecdotes,* 1966

All gardeners live in beautiful places because they make them so.

—JOSEPH JOUBERT, *Pensées,* 1838

Half the interest of a garden is the constant exercise of the imagination.

—MRS. C. W. [THERESA] EARLE,
Pot-pourri from a Surrey Garden, 1897

A swarm of bees in May is worth a load of hay;
a swarm of bees in June is worth a silver spoon;
but a swarm in July is not worth a fly.

—ENGLISH PROVERB

Don't wear perfume in the garden—unless you want to be pollinated by bees.

—ANNE RAVER (b. 1949)

His Labor is a Chant—
His Idleness—a Tune—
Oh, for a Bee's experience
Of Clovers, and of Noon!

—EMILY DICKINSON, "No. 916," ca. 1864

I imagine my Victorian great-grandmother, perpetually dressed in black taffeta with a bonnet on her head (as far as I can tell from the single photograph that has come down to me), ensconced in a wicker chair beside a trellis of roses and leaving it to the bees to demonstrate to her five children how they had come to be.

—SARA STEIN, *My Weeds,* 1988

Once some friends of mine bought a lakeside cottage that had been unoccupied for several years, and discovered that the walls were full of bees. They appealed to me for help, so I assembled my [bee-hunting] gear and went after them. . . . An unbelievable amount of honey was stored there, some of it a year or more old and completely crystallized. I obtained more than a hundred pounds of this finest of sweets from this one venture.

—EUELL GIBBONS, *Stalking the Wild Asparagus,* 1962

The possessor of a four-leafed Clover is proof against any witchcraft which may be attempted against him; and if a maiden place such a clover in her left shoe, the first man she meets, or his brother, will become her husband.

—A. STODDARD KULL, *Secrets of Flowers,* 1976

It always seems to me that the herbaceous peony [*Paeonia lactiflora,* Chinese peony] is the very epitome of June. Larger than any rose, it has something of the cabbage rose's voluminous quality; and when it finally drops from the vase, it sheds its vast petticoats with a bump on the table, all in an intact heap, much as a rose will suddenly fall, making us look up from our book or conversation, to notice for one moment the death of what had still appeared to be a living beauty.

—VITA SACKVILLE-WEST, *Garden Book,* 1968

Eleven at night. I am just come out of the garden in the most oriental of all evenings, and from breathing odours beyond those of Araby. The acacias, which the Arabians have the sense to worship, are covered with blossoms, the honeysuckles dangle from every tree in festoons, the seringas are thickets of sweets, and the new-cut hay in the field tempers the balmy gales with simple freshness; while a thousand sky-rockets launched into the air at Ranelagh or Marybone illuminate the scene, and give it an air of Haroun Alraschid's paradise.

—HORACE WALPOLE, letter, 10 June 1765

The distilled water [of the strawberry] drunke with white Wine is good against the passion of the heart, reviving the spirits, and making the heart merry.

—JOHN GERARD, *The Herball,* 1633

One June, while canoeing on Rancocas Creek in New Jersey, I noticed the small creeping plants [of wild cranberry], with their tiny leaves and pale, rose-colored flowers, growing in a creekside bog. I noted the location and have returned there each year, to gather as many cranberries as my family can use.

—EUELL GIBBONS, *Stalking the Wild Asparagus,* 1962

I wish I knew half what the flock of them know
Of where all the berries and other things grow,
Cranberries in bogs and raspberries on top
Of the boulder-strewn mountain, and when they
    will crop.

—ROBERT FROST (1874-1963), "Blueberries"

MIDSUMMER, 24 JUNE

At Midsommer, downe with the brembles and
    brakes,
and after, abrode with thy forks and thy rakes:
Set mowers a mowing, where meadow is growne,
the longer now standing the worse to be mowne.

—THOMAS TUSSER,
A Hundreth Good Pointes of Husbandrie, 1557

LORD ILLINGWORTH: The Book of Life begins with
a man and a woman in a garden.
MRS. ALLONBY: It ends with Revelations.

—OSCAR WILDE, *A Woman of No Importance,* 1893

Chasing the naughty couples down the grass-green gooseberried double bed of the wood.

—DYLAN THOMAS, *Under Milk Wood,* 1954

I have a garden of my own,
Shining with flow'rs of ev'ry hue;
I lov'd it dearly while alone,
But I shall love it more with you.

—THOMAS MOORE (1779-1852), "I Have a Garden"

ST. PAUL'S DAY, 29 JUNE

If St. Paul's Day be fair and clear,
it will betide a happy year.

—ENGLISH PROVERB

He had been eight years upon a project for extracting sun-beams out of cucumbers, which were to be put in-to vials hermetically sealed, and let out to warm the air in raw inclement summers.

–JONATHAN SWIFT, *Gulliver's Travels,* 1726

July

It's a sure sign of summer if the chair gets up when you do.

—Walter Winchell (1897-1972)

One of the minor tragedies of my boyhood, which seems ludicrous now, occurred when I threw a rock into the top of a mulberry, then rushed under the tree to get some of the dislodged fruit before the other children beat me to it, and was struck in the back of the head by the same stone I had thrown.

—Euell Gibbons, *Stalking the Wild Asparagus,* 1962

The poetry of earth is never dead:
When all the birds are faint with the hot sun,
And hide in cooling trees, a voice will run
From hedge to hedge about the new-mown mead.

—JOHN KEATS,
"On the Grasshopper and Cricket," 1817

Of all the plants I know, the one whose foliage has the strongest sound is the Virginian allspice (*Calycanthus floridus*), whose leaves are of so dry and harsh a quality that they seem to grate and clash as they come together.

—GERTRUDE JEKYLL, *Home and Garden,* 1900

All night have the roses heard
The flute, violin, bassoon;
All night has the casement jessamine stirr'd
To the dancers dancing in tune;
Till a silence fell with the waking bird,
And a hush with the setting moon.

—ALFRED, LORD TENNYSON, "Maud," 1855

There was a garden and in the middle of the garden was a tree. There was a platform under the tree made of trunks and slabs; and there... two girls sat to watch the garden and sing watch-garden songs. They did this to make the garden grow, just as people sing to a baby to make it be quiet and feel good. In old times we sang to a garden for a like reason, to make the garden feel good and grow.

—BUFFALO BIRD WOMAN, in Gilbert L. Wilson, *Buffalo Bird Woman's Garden,* 1917

The sun is coming down to earth, and the fields and the waters shout to him golden shouts.

—GEORGE MEREDITH, *The Ordeal of Richard Feverel,* 1859

A slight sound at evening lifts me up by the ears, and makes life seem inexpressibly serene and grand. It may be in Uranus, or it may be in the shutter.

—HENRY DAVID THOREAU, journal, 10-12 July 1841

If we had better hearing, and could discern the descants of sea birds, the rhythmic tympani of schools of mollusks, or even the distant harmonics of midges hanging over meadows in the sun, the combined sound might lift us off our feet.

—LEWIS THOMAS, *The Lives of a Cell,* 1974

ST. SWITHIN'S DAY, 15 JULY

St. Swithin's Day, if thou dost rain,
for forty days it will remain;
St. Swithin's Day, if thou be fair,
for forty days 'twill rain nae mair.

—ENGLISH PROVERB

Every one of us must have inherited a bit of a farmer in his blood, even if we have no geraniums or sea-onions growing outside our windows, for when the sun has shone steadily for a week we look anxiously at the sky and say to one another as we meet, "It ought to rain."

—KAREL Čapek, *The Gardener's Year,* 1929

Rain before seven, fine before eleven.

—ENGLISH PROVERB

Gather the unopened flower buds [of *Hemerocallis fulva,* orange day-lily] when they are nearly full-sized, boil only a few minutes, then butter, season and serve like green beans. They are really delicious, with no bad taste of any kind.

—EUELL GIBBONS, *Stalking the Wild Asparagus,* 1962

Our sea-walled garden, the whole land,
Is full of weeds, her fairest flowers choked up,
Her fruit-trees all unpruned, her hedges ruined,
Her knots disordered, and her wholesome herbs
Swarming with caterpillars.

—WILLIAM SHAKESPEARE, *Richard II,* 1595

ORGANIC GARLIC-OIL PESTICIDE

Grind up in a blender 24 ounces of garlic and mix well with 16 teaspoons of mineral oil. Let stand 24 hours. Dissolve 2 ounces of Ivory soap shavings in 1 gallon of water. Add garlic-oil mixture and let stand overnight. Mix well. Strain through a cloth. Add 1 part of this mixture to 10 parts of water in a sprayer and apply to plants weekly. If insects are already present, use every 3 days for control, and then weekly thereafter. Mix a fresh batch for each application.

–Recipe sent by plantsman ROBERT D. RODGERS to seed wholesalers George J. Ball Inc.

Perennials are the ones that grow like weeds, biennials are the ones that die this year instead of next, and hardy annuals are the ones that never come up at all.

–KATHARINE WHITEHORN, *Observations,* 1970

In gardening I have one gift
You won't find in manuals:
I know it's strange,
But I can change
Perennials into annuals.

—ANONYMOUS

By the end of July I have had it with weeds and gardens. The optimism needed to motivate the care of a hundred infant azaleas that won't begin to resemble nature for a decade fails me. The cutting down of spent veronica and seedy mallow reveals crabgrass and ragweed that had been hidden by the blooming crowd.

—SARA STEIN, *My Weeds,* 1988

You may drive out Nature with a pitchfork, yet she'll be constantly running back.

—HORACE (65-8 B.C.), *Epistles*

I've had enough of gardening—I'm just about ready to throw in the trowel.

—ANONYMOUS

A farm is an irregular patch of nettles bounded by short-term notes, containing a fool and his wife who didn't know enough to stay in the city.

—S. J. PERELMAN (1904-79)

A good farmer is nothing more nor less than a handy man with a sense of humus.

—E. B. WHITE, *One Man's Meat,* 1944

August

DOG DAYS, CA. 3 JULY TO CA. 15 AUGUST

Shut, shut the door, good John! (fatigu'd, I said);
Tie up the knocker! say I'm sick, I'm dead.
The Dog-star rages!

—ALEXANDER POPE,
"An Epistle to Dr. Arbuthnot," 1735

Remember
When we last gathered roses in the garden,
I found my wits; but truly you lost yours.

—JOHN FORD, *The Broken Heart,* ca. 1628

CALMATIVE HERBAL BATH

For overly nervous and hysteric persons. Mix together a small handful each of camomile, hops, linden, cannabis, yarrow, valerian, and passion-flower. Simmer in a quart of water for 10 minutes. Sip ½ cup of the liquid with a little lemon and honey and pour the rest in your bathtub. Soak for at least 30 minutes.

—JEANNE ROSE, *Herbs and Things,* 1972

There is a garden in her face
Where roses and white lilies grow;
A heavenly paradise is that place
Wherein all pleasant fruits do flow.

—THOMAS CAMPION, *Fourth Book of Airs,* 1617

Her cheeks so rare a white was on,
No daisy makes comparison
(Who sees them is undone),
For streaks of red were mingled there,
Such as are on a Catherine pear
(The side that's next the sun).
Her lips were red, and one was thin
Compared to that was next her chin
(Some bee had stung her newly).

—JOHN SUCKLING, "A Ballad upon a Wedding," 1646

She could never forget that the man she loved was a man with a past. He had been a poet. Deep down in her soul there was always the corroding fear lest at any moment a particularly fine sunset or the sight of a rose in bud might undo all the work she had done, sending Rodney hot-foot once more to his Thesaurus and rhyming dictionary. It was for this reason that she always hurried him indoors when the sun began to go down and refused to have rose trees in her garden.

—P. G. WODEHOUSE, *Nothing Serious,* 1950

Gather in August [while the sun is in Leo] the Heliotropon, wrap it in a Bay-leaf with a wolf's tooth, and it will, if placed under the pillow, show a man who has been robbed where are his goods, and who has taken them. Also, if placed in a church, it will keep fixed in their places all the women present who have broken their marriage vows. This last is most tried and most true.

—ALBERTUS MAGNUS (CA. 1206–80)

It is a sad moment when the first phlox appears. It is the amber light indicating the end of the great burst of early summer and suggesting that we must now start looking forward to autumn. Not that I have any objection to autumn as a season, full of its own beauty; but I just cannot bear to see another summer go, and I recoil from what the first hint of autumn means.

—VITA SACKVILLE-WEST, *Garden Book,* 1968

ST. BARTHOLOMEW'S DAY, 24 AUGUST

If St. Bartholomew's Day be fair and clear,
then a prosperous autumn comes that year.

—ENGLISH PROVERB

Violets smell like burnt sugar cubes that have been dipped in lemon and velvet.

—DIANE ACKERMAN,
A Natural History of the Senses, 1990

That [flower] which above all others yields the sweetest smell in the air, is the violet, specially the white double violet, which comes twice a year; about the middle of April, and about Bartholomew-tide.

—FRANCIS BACON, "Of Gardens," 1625

A garland of Violets, worn about the head, prevents dizziness.

—A. STODDARD KULL, *Secrets of Flowers,* 1976

How cunningly nature hides every wrinkle of her inconceivable antiquity under roses and violets and morning dew!

—RALPH WALDO EMERSON,
Letters and Social Aims, 1876

But though an old man, I am but a young gardener.

—THOMAS JEFFERSON, letter, 20 August 1811

When I used to pick the berries for dinner on the East Quarter hills I did not eat one till I had done, for going a-berrying implies more things than eating the berries. They at home got only the pudding: I got the forenoon out of doors and the appetite for the pudding.

—HENRY DAVID THOREAU, journal, 22 August 1860

As to the garden, it seems to me its chief fruit is—blackbirds.

—WILLIAM MORRIS, letter, 24 August 1888

I saw the spiders marching through air,
Swimming from tree to tree that mildewed day
In latter August when the hay
Came creaking into the barn.

—ROBERT LOWELL,
"Mr. Edwards and the Spider," 1946

September

September...what a turnover, what a watershed of the year.

—VITA SACKVILLE-WEST, *More for Your Garden*, 1955

What wondrous life is this I lead!
Ripe apples drop about my head;
The luscious clusters of the vine
Upon my mouth do crush their wine;
The nectarine and curious peach
Into my hands themselves do reach;
Stumbling on melons as I pass,
Insnared with flowers, I fall on grass.

—ANDREW MARVELL, "The Garden," 1681

Into the breast that gives the rose
Shall I with shuddering fall!

—George Meredith,
"The Spirit of Earth in Autumn," 1862

September blowe soft, till fruite be in loft.

—Thomas Tusser,
A Hundreth Good Pointes of Husbandrie, 1557

LABOR DAY

Blessèd are the horny hands of toil!

—James Russell Lowell, "A Glance Behind the Curtain," in *Democratic Review,* September 1843

Blessed be agriculture! If one does not have too much of it.

—Charles Dudley Warner,
My Summer in a Garden, 1871

Good seed makes a good crop.

—English proverb

It matters little comparatively whether the fields fill the farmer's barn. The true husbandman will cease from anxiety, as the squirrels manifest no concern whether the woods will bear chestnuts this year or not, and finish his labor with every day, relinquishing all claim to the produce of his fields, and sacrificing in his mind not only his first but his last fruits also.

—HENRY DAVID THOREAU, *Walden,* 1854

Good huswives in summer will save their own
seedes
Against the next yere—as occasion needes.
One seede for another, to make an exchange
With fellowlie neighbourhood seemeth not strange.

—THOMAS TUSSER,
A Hundreth Good Pointes of Husbandrie, 1557

In my father's family we often sold a good deal of seed in the spring to families that wanted. The price was one tanned buffalo skin for one string of braided seed corn.

—BUFFALO BIRD WOMAN, in Gilbert L. Wilson,
Buffalo Bird Woman's Garden, 1917

Stolen fruit is sweet.

—ENGLISH PROVERB

Stolen sweets are always sweeter,
Stolen kisses much completer,
Stolen looks are nice in chapels,
Stolen, stolen, be your apples.

—LEIGH HUNT,
"Song of Fairies Robbing an Orchard," 1830

CURE FOR WARTS

Steal an apple, and cut it into as many pieces as you have warts. Rub each piece of the apple on each wart and wrap the pieces in an old cloth. Bury the cloth. When the apple bits have rotted, the warts will be gone.

—JEANNE ROSE, *Herbs and Things,* 1972

The next day after the corn was plucked, we gave a husking feast.... The husking season was looked upon as a time of jollity; and youths and maidens dressed and decked themselves for the occasion.

—BUFFALO BIRD WOMAN, in Gilbert L. Wilson, *Buffalo Bird Woman's Garden,* 1917

The fruit [of *Rosa eglanteria,* eglantine or sweet-brier] when it is ripe maketh most pleasant meats and banqueting dishes, as tarts and such like; the making whereof I commit to the cunning cooke, and teeth to eat them in the rich mans mouth.

—JOHN GERARD, *The Herball,* 1633

The lovely Saffron Crocus [*Crocus sativus*] was the exclusive joy of the rajah of Kashmir for many years. In the time of Edward III, however, a fore-handed English traveler secreted one of the bulbs of the plant in a hollow staff, and so brought the flower to the West.

—A. STODDARD KULL, *Secrets of Flowers,* 1976

Flowers have spoken to me more than I can tell in written words. They are the hieroglyphics of angels, loved by all men for the beauty of the character, though few can decypher even fragments of their meaning.

—LYDIA M. CHILD, letter, 1 September 1842

I just come and talk to the plants, really—very important to talk to them, they respond I find.

—CHARLES, PRINCE OF WALES,
television interview, 21 September 1986

A walk in the woods is only an exalted dream.

—RALPH WALDO EMERSON,
journal, 29 September 1839

I have a hut in the wood, none knows it but my Lord; an ash tree this side, a hazel on the other, a great tree on a mound encloses it. Two heathery door-posts for support, and a lintel of honeysuckle; around its close the wood sheds its mits upon fat swine. The size of my hut, small yet not small, a place of familiar paths, the she-bird in its dress of blackbird colour sings a melodious strain from its gable.

—IRISH, 10th century

A harvest moon!
And on the mats—
Shadows of pine boughs.

—KIKAKU (1661-1707), "Harvest Moon"

October

O suns and skies and clouds of June,
And flowers of June together,
Ye cannot rival for one hour
October's bright blue weather.

—HELEN HUNT JACKSON (1830–85),
"October's Bright Blue Weather"

Blue evening falls,
Blue evening falls;
Nearby in every direction,
It sets the corn tassels trembling.

—SONG OF THE PAPAGO INDIANS

Hedge-crickets sing; and now with treble soft
The red-breast whistles from a garden-croft;
And gathering swallows twitter in the skies.

—JOHN KEATS, "To Autumn," 1820

The scarlet of the maples can shake me like a cry
Of bugles going by.
And my lonely spirit thrills
To see the frosty asters like a smoke upon the hills.

—BLISS CARMAN, "A Vagabond Song," 1894

The lost leaves measure our years; they are gone as the days are gone.

—RICHARD JEFFERIES, *The Life of the Fields,* 1908

In October dung your field
and your land its wealth shall yield.

—ENGLISH PROVERB

ST. LUKE'S DAY, 18 OCTOBER

On St. Luke's Day, the pumpkins go stale.

—VENETIAN SAYING

Who can endure a cabbage bed in October?

—JANE AUSTEN, *Sandition,* written 1817

For man, autumn is a time of harvest, of gathering together. For nature, it is a time of sowing, of scattering abroad.

—EDWIN WAY TEALE, *Autumn Across America,* 1956

Give me handfuls of lilies to scatter.

—VIRGIL (70–19 B.C.), *Aeneid*

Things often get out of proportion in a garden. Therefore in autumn the shifting of flowers is performed; every year the gardener carries his perennials about like a cat her kittens; every year he says with satisfaction: So, now I have it all planted and in order. Next year he sighs with the same satisfaction. A garden is never finished. In that sense it is like the human world and all human undertakings.

—KAREL ČAPEK, *The Gardener's Year,* 1929

Gardening is largely a question of mixing one sort of plant with another sort of plant, and of seeing how they marry happily together; and if you see that they don't marry happily, then you must hoick one of them out and be quite ruthless about it. That is the only way to garden. The true gardener must be brutal, and imaginative for the future.

—VITA SACKVILLE-WEST, *Garden Book,* 1968

A garden is always a series of losses set against a few triumphs, like life itself.

—MAY SARTON, *At Seventy,* 1984

The love of gardening is a seed that once sown never dies, but always grows and grows to an enduring and ever-increasing source of happiness.

—GERTRUDE JEKYLL, *Wood and Garden,* 1899

The trouble with gardening is that it does not remain an avocation. It becomes an obsession.

—PHYLLIS MCGINLEY (1905–78)

One hears a lot about the rules of good husbandry; there is only one–leave the land far better than you found it.

–GEORGE HENDERSON, *The Farming Ladder,* 1944

A springful of larks in a rolling
Cloud and the roadside bushes brimming with
    whistling
Black birds and the sun of October
Summery
On the hill's shoulder, . . .
There could I marvel
My birthday
Away but the weather turned around.

–DYLAN THOMAS, "Poem in October," 1946

A change in the weather is sufficient to recreate the world and ourselves.

–MARCEL PROUST,
Remembrance of Things Past, 1921

Nature has no mercy at all. Nature says, "I'm going to snow. If you have on a bikini and no snow-shoes, that's tough. I am going to snow anyway."

—MAYA ANGELOU, interview, October 1974

HALLOWEEN, 31 OCTOBER

Only the knife knows what goes on in the heart of a pumpkin.

—SIMONE SCHWARZ-BART,
The Bridge of Beyond, 1972

November

No shade, no shine, no butterflies, no bees,
No fruits, no flowers, no leaves, no birds,–
November!

–THOMAS HOOD, "No!," 1844

Signs of decay, of imminent death, come as a relief after a fruitful season, and the sinister words "killing frost" hold no terrors for me. It will all begin again, soon enough.

–ELEANOR PERÉNYI, *Green Thoughts*, 1981

Earth knows no desolation. She smells regeneration in the moist breath of decay.

–GEORGE MEREDITH (1828-1909)

One thing that unites all gardeners as they contemplate the compost heap is a belief in reincarnation, at least for plants.

—GEOFFREY CHARLESWORTH,
The Opinionated Gardener, 1988

Beyond the window-pane the chill of autumn frost is in the air. Proud herbs of summer are collapsed.... Soon the twigs of bushes will be laden with snow. Yet here my potted plants are lively and brilliant with the sunshine of milder climes.

—LIBERTY HYDE BAILEY,
How Plants Get Their Names, 1933

Who loves a garden, loves a green-house too,
Unconscious of a less propitious clime
There blooms exotic beauty, warm and snug,
While the winds whistle and the snows descend.

—WILLIAM COWPER, *The Task,* 1785

There are only three things that can kill a farmer: lightning, rolling over in a tractor, and old age.

—BILL BRYSON, *Notes from a Small Island,* 1995

Life is nothing. Life is all. It is the hand with which we hold off death. It is the glow-worm that shines in the night-time and is black in the morning; it is the white breath of the oxen in winter; it is the little shadow that runs across the grass and loses itself at sunset.

—H. RIDER HAGGARD, *King Solomon's Mines,* 1886

I want death to find me planting my cabbages, but caring little for it, and even less about the imperfections of my garden.

—MONTAIGNE, *Essais,* 1580

A rose in flower is, so to speak, only for dilettanti; the gardener's pleasure is deeper rooted, right in the womb of the soil. After his death the gardener does not become a butterfly, intoxicated by the perfumes of flowers, but a garden worm tasting all the dark, nitrogenous, and spicy delights of the soil.

—KAREL ČAPEK, *The Gardener's Year,* 1929

I bequeath myself to the dirt to grow from the
    grass I love,
If you want me again look for me under your
    boot-soles.

—WALT WHITMAN, "Song of Myself," 1891-92

AGE-DEFYING BEAUTY BATH

Take a handful of dried Lavender flowers, a handful of Rosemary leaves, handful of dried Mint, handful of Comfrey roots, and one of Thyme. Mix all together loosely in a muslin bag. Place in your bath, pour on enough boiling water to cover and let soak ten minutes. Then fill up tub. Rest fifteen minutes in the "magic water"—and think virtuous thoughts.

—NINON DE LENCLOS (1620-1705),
in Joseph E. Meyer, *The Herbalist,* 1918

The root [of radish] stamped with hony and the powder of a sheepes heart dried, causeth haire to grow in short space.

—JOHN GERARD, *The Herball,* 1633

There is, of course, a gold mine or a buried treasure on every mortgaged homestead. Whether the farmer ever digs for it or not, it is there, haunting his daydreams when the burden of debt is most unbearable.

—FAWN BRODIE, *No Man Knows My History,* 1945

A gardener must not feel sorry for himself, even in winter, and no matter how great the cause.

—HENRY MITCHELL, *The Essential Earthman,* 1981

Whoever could make two ears of corn, or two blades of grass, to grow upon a spot of ground where only one grew before, would deserve better of mankind, and do more essential service to his country, than the whole race of politicians put together.

—JONATHAN SWIFT, *Gulliver's Travels,* 1726

Give fools their gold, and knaves their power;
Let fortune's bubbles rise and fall;
Who sows a field, or trains a flower,
Or plants a tree, is more than all.

—JOHN GREENLEAF WHITTIER (1807–92),
"A Song of Harvest"

In the fall, when we went to our winter lodges, corn, squash, beans, and whatever else was needed, we loaded on our horses and took with us. As soon as we came to our winter lodge we made ready a cache pit [root cellar] at once and stored these things away.

—BUFFALO BIRD WOMAN, in Gilbert L. Wilson, *Buffalo Bird Woman's Garden,* 1917

THANKSGIVING

Come, ye thankful people, come,
Raise the song of harvest-home;
All is safely gathered in,
Ere the winter storms begin.

—HENRY ALFORD,
"Come, Ye Thankful People, Come," 1844

If the dining room be sprinkled with water in which the herbe [vervain] hath been steeped the guests will be the merrier.

—PLINY THE ELDER (A.D. 23-79), *Historia Naturalis*

A New Englander, who thought his Brandied Rum Cherries were especially good, decided, after some hesitation, to give a jar of them to his minister. He waited with much trepidation for the preacher's comment. Finally he received a little thank-you note which read: "Dear Parishioner, You can't imagine how delighted I was to receive your little present. But what I appreciated even more than the gift was the *spirit* in which it was given."

—EUELL GIBBONS, *Stalking the Wild Asparagus,* 1962

The night is freezing fast,
To-morrow comes December.

—A. E. HOUSMAN (1859-1936),
"The Night Is Freezing Fast"

December

In drear nighted December
Too happy, happy tree
Thy branches ne'er remember
Their green felicity.

—John Keats, "In Drear Nighted December," written 1817

I have forgotten much, but still remember
The poinsettia's red, blood-red in warm December.

—Claude McKay (1890-1948), "Flame-Heart"

Ah, dear nature, the mere remembrance, after a short forgetfulness, of the pine woods! I come to it as a hungry man to a crust of bread.

—Henry David Thoreau, journal, 12 December 1851

There is wood as far as one can see, here mostly of the silver-stemmed Birch and rich green Holly, with the woodland carpet of dusky low-toned bramble and quiet, dead leaf and brilliant moss.

—GERTRUDE JEKYLL, *Wood and Garden,* 1899

ST. THOMAS' DAY, 21 DECEMBER

St. Thomas divine: brewing, baking, and skilling of fat swine.

—ENGLISH PROVERB

SATURNALIA, 17 TO 24 DECEMBER

The great feast of Saturn was held in December, when the people decorated the temples with such green things as they could find.... The pagan Romans used to send to their friends holly-sprigs, during the Saturnalia, with wishes for their health and well-being.

—E. COBHAM BREWER,
Dictionary of Phrase and Fable, 1898

Then stick up ivy and the bays,
And then restore the heathen ways,
Green will remind you of the Spring.

—HENRY VAUGHAN (1622-95), "The True Christmas"

Heigh-ho! sing, heigh-ho! unto the green holly:
Most friendship is feigning, most loving mere folly:
Then heigh-ho! the holly!
This life is most jolly.

—WILLIAM SHAKESPEARE, *As You Like It,* 1599

On Christmas eve, and yesterday, there were little branches of misletoe hanging in several parts of our house, in the kitchen, the entries, the parlor, and the smoking room—suspended from the gas-fittings. The maids of the house did their utmost to entrap the gentlemen-boarders, old and young, under these privileged places, and there to kiss them, after which they were expected to pay a shilling.

—NATHANIEL HAWTHORNE, *English Notebooks,* 1870

I can never remember whether it snowed for six days and six nights when I was twelve or whether it snowed for twelve days and twelve nights when I was six.

—DYLAN THOMAS, *A Child's Christmas in Wales,* 1954

Snowy winter, plentiful harvest.

—VERMONT SAYING

We are nearer to Spring
Than we were in September,
I heard a bird sing
In the dark of December.

—OLIVER HERFORD (1863-1935), "I Heard a Bird Sing"

And since to look at things in bloom
Fifty springs are little room,
About the woodlands I will go
To see the cherry hung with snow.

—A. E. HOUSMAN, *A Shropshire Lad,* 1896

Therefore all seasons shall be sweet to thee,
Whether the summer clothe the general earth
With greenness, or the redbreast sit and sing
Betwixt the tufts of snow on the bare branch
Of mossy apple-tree.

—SAMUEL TAYLOR COLERIDGE,
"Frost at Midnight," 1798

A gardener, perhaps more than anyone else, is aware of the change of seasons and the passage of time. While time may pass most pleasantly in a garden, we know that each of us will have the chance to make only a certain number of gardens. I count each year as another garden, and each fall wistfully acknowledge that another will be gone soon. Gardening is a daily, yearly, and lifelong practice.

—ROB PROCTOR, *Perennials,* 1990

We gardeners live somehow for the future; if roses are in flower, we think that next year they will flower better; and in some few years this little spruce will become a tree–if only those few years were behind me! I should like to see what these birches will be like in fifty years.

–KAREL ČAPEK, *The Gardener's Year,* 1929

I cannot help hoping that the great ghostly barn-owl will sweep silently across a pale garden, next summer, in the twilight–the pale garden that I am now planting, under the first flakes of snow.

–VITA SACKVILLE-WEST, *Garden Book,* 1968

A garden is never so good as it will be next year.

–THOMAS COOPER,
in *Horticulture Magazine,* January 1993